Do As I Do

Using Social Learning to Train Dogs

Claudia Fugazza

Dogwise™ Publishing

Wenatchee, Washington, U.S.A.

Do As I Do
Using Social Learning to Train Dogs
Claudia Fugazza

Dogwise Publishing
A Division of Direct Book Service, Inc.
403 South Mission Street, Wenatchee, Washington 98801
1-509-663-9115, 1-800-776-2665
www.dogwisepublishing.com / info@dogwisepublishing.com

Original version of this book and dvd entitled Do As I Do, Il cane impara guardandoci was published in Italy by Haqihana in 2011.
© 2014 Claudia Fugazza. English language version of book and DVD published by Dogwise Publishing with permission of Haqihana.
Photos: Claudia Fugazza and Federica Lazza. Reprinted with permission of Haqihana.
Graphic design: Lindsay Peternell

Library of Congress Cataloging-in-Publication Data
Fugazza, Claudia, 1978-
  Do as I do : using social learning to train dogs / by Claudia Fugazza.
    pages cm
  Includes index.
  ISBN 978-1-61781-148-7
  1. Dogs--Training. 2. Dogs--Psychology. 3. Social learning. I. Title.
  SF431.F84 2014
  636.7'0835--dc23
                                    2014014123

ISBN: 978-1-61781-148-7

Printed in the U.S.A.

Dedication

This book is dedicated to my beloved India, life companion and soul mate, friend and eternal source of inspiration.

The intimate bond we shared for years, the experiences and promises, the memories mutually interwoven render living without you even more difficult.

However, it was precisely from what existed between the two of us that grew the ideas and thoughts behind my research. This book also exists because of you.

Nacchera, you will always live within me.

Table of Contents

Acknowledgments

An immense thank you (and a tasty reward) to India for embarking on this journey with me, and to all the dogs and owners who have participated in our studies for allowing us to discover a bit of their minds.

I am also grateful to my mother, whose literary skills greatly contributed to improving the draft of this book.

A special acknowledgment goes to Professor Adam Miklósi from the Ethology Department at the University of Budapest for helping me to elaborate the various projects within my research line.

And last but not least thank you to my partner for supporting me and standing with me while I was so busy with my research that I even forgot about eating.

Foreword

There are two types of people in the world. Some of them believe that dogs are not able to imitate humans; others are convinced that dogs readily copy human behavior. Perhaps this is the place where I should admit that I had belonged to the former group of people for many years, before József Topál and I dared to test this idea of imitation in dogs for the first time, some years ago. I did not have much to lose—being a non-believer anyway—so it came to me as a huge surprise that Philip, a well-trained Belgian Shepherd assistance dog for the disabled, showed clear signs of imitation abilities after some weeks of training.

I also have vivid memories about getting back the reviewers' comments on our first draft paper describing the Do As I Do method and the impressive results with Philip. Their comments were longer than the manuscript, and of course it was clear that these fellow researchers were non-believers—like me—so it is highly likely that I would have also been critical if I had been in the same situation. But Philip's performance did not leave room for any doubt! A few years later we managed to train some more dogs by means of the same method, the result being that there was no doubt that these other dogs were able to show functional imitation of human behavior without any special training, just like Philip.

Although I came to think that the Do As I Do method could be a useful way to extend the training of dogs (and owners), it was Claudia Fugazza's courage and persistence that was the key factor in developing this new method for the wider dog-loving audience. I hope this book is only the first step to introduce the Do As I Do method to dog trainers and dog owners, and I am sure that Claudia will have many more ideas to develop this method further and further. This book provides a very nice and helpful introduction to the concept of social learning and also explains in detail how Do As I Do training should be performed.

I have always been a bit annoyed that dog training—as the term implies—focuses on the dog, while actually it should be about synchronization of the behavior of dog and owner. Just like dancing is not about man-training (most women have a natural talent for dancing anyway!) but is about learning how to move together in a synchronized fashion. The same applies to the Do As I Do method. Owners or trainers become equal partners with their dogs, and they can experience and feel what the execution of a specific action means for their companion. Relying on the Do As I Do method gives dog training a real social flavor, makes it more enjoyable and more fun.

Apart from this, the Do As I Do method offers an easy way to teach new types of actions with relatively little effort on the part of the dog. They may not be able to execute behaviors precisely the first time, but you can see they can grasp the concept. Claudia Fugazza and I showed that this method is at least as good as other, traditional methods of dog training. And there is no need to abandon your old methods; just teach Do As I Do to your dog as a complementary way of social interaction.

Let me end by sharing a new idea with you. By watching puppies interact with each other, you can see how much they want to engage in group activities, including performing similar actions that they see the other puppies perform. Based on this, I have come to believe that the way dogs learn from each other is a basic skill activated very early in development. The main problem is that, in most cases, we humans get them out of this habit by not encouraging such activities. Dogs should not dig when the owner is digging or open the refrigerator after seeing the owner doing it! So the Do As I Do method simply awakens a natural skill in the dog and puts some human control over his synchronizing tendencies. Thus dogs who are allowed to imitate their owners will love doing it and have a happier life…so give it a try… You can do it…as we did!

Adam Miklósi, Professor of Ethology
Family Dog Project, Budapest, Hungary

Introduction

I made the decision to write this book in order to help spread a new training method that takes advantage of the social learning skills of dogs and their predisposition to learn by observing, and then imitating and/or repeating behaviors, performed by humans. Interestingly, despite the fact it is now well known that dogs have excellent social learning skills, training methods used so far have not relied on their ability to learn by observation and imitation.

Traditionally, the techniques used for dog training have been based on individual associative learning, that is, operant and classical (Pavlovian) conditioning. Almost every species has the skill to learn, e.g., through association, even very simple organisms as well as those who do not live in complex social structures like packs and families. But I have always been curious to know if my dogs learn to open doors on their own by simple associative learning, for instance by trial and error, or whether it is by a different process reflecting their eminently social nature and their great observational skills. I am sure that many dog owners have noticed the inclination of dogs to be curious and attracted toward what we humans do and the objects we handle. How many of us have bedded plants out in the garden with great care under a dog's scrutiny, digging a small hole, introducing the roots and lovingly covering them with fresh soil, only to find out later on that the dog has pulled the plants out and perhaps even meticulously dug up the entire garden. While we were digging, Fido probably thought that it was an interesting game and that he wanted his share of the fun. It seems to me that the question that needs to be addressed is whether dogs can learn through the use of social learning, observing and then replicating the actions of their human companions.

In this book you will be introduced to social learning through the use of a training protocol known as "Do As I Do." The accompanying DVD complements the book in that it illustrates the steps of the protocol with examples that will prove useful when practicing together with your dog. My advice is that you first read the corresponding section of the book before watching the illustrative examples contained in the DVD.

1
Discovering a New Way
to Learn and Train

As a way of introducing the subject of this book, allow me to tell the story about how I first learned about the potential of social learning and the Do As I Do protocol.

Siria and the water faucet

Siria was my Czechoslovakian Wolfdog with an awesome silver-colored coat. My favorite portrait of her and her amber eyes hangs in my sitting room. However, the fondest memory I keep of her is the way she used to wake me up in the morning with licks, her sweet greeting ritual. Siria was not only a great dog, but she also marked a course change in my life.

It happens sometimes that the drive to study the behavior of companion animals stems from the little seed of a routine episode. In this case, my curiosity was so strong that it led me to abandon my previous profession in order to start studying dog ethology.

One night, after an intense working day, I was exhausted and could not wait to pick up the book that rested on my bedside table, read a few pages and then go to sleep. It was right at the moment when I began to relax that I heard a noise in the background. I had no idea where it came from. Was it the radio in the bathroom? It was like the white noise from a radio out of tune. However, I was positive that I had switched off my radio.

After paying closer attention, I realized that it was the sound of water coming out of a faucet. I got up from my bed and went to check the bathroom. I was convinced that I had shut the water off completely. However, a small stream of water was pouring out of the faucet. I turned it off and went back to bed.

The same thing happened the next night. So I tried to come up with an explanation for what seemed to be just a coincidence. Was it perhaps the fatigue of the day and the fact that I was in a hurry to get to bed that made me forget to shut off the faucet in the sink properly? I thought about when I had last turned the water on. Siria had in fact asked me to do it with a subtle paw touch, her signal to me that she would like a drink. She loved drinking water straight from the tap and I gave in to her desire and over time it became a sort of evening ritual for both of us. However, I was pretty sure that I had closed it that night. In fact I was positive I had, because a little later Siria approached me to ask me to open it again. I had been busy replying to some messages, so I let her understand that the fun was over for the night.

Had Siria opened the faucet by herself? Was it possible that she had learned how to do it after observing me performing the same maneuver so many times? On my way to bed, I reflected on the fact that Siria had already learned to open the doors at my house, most likely through observation. While opening the faucet was definitely more difficult, there was a possibility that she had learned how to do it by observing me.

Now I had a theory to test. When Siria asked me for help to open the faucet the next day, I did not do it and waited to observe her behavior. She insisted several times: "You have always done this for me…Why are you now pretending that you do not understand what I want?" Finally I left the bathroom, resigned to the conclusion that it was me who had forgotten to close the faucet properly the past couple days. However, as I walked away, I noticed that Siria went back into the bathroom without me.

I decided to sneak in and spy on her so that she would not notice my presence. I was surprised to watch her pressing her nose on the faucet until water came out and she was able to drink. It was this episode that pushed me to do my first research on social learning.

Philip and India
After I was convinced that Siria had learned to open a water faucet by imitating me, my curiosity pushed me to dig into the scientific literature and to read just about everything I could on social learning in dogs as well as other species. It became evident that there was no consensus in the literature. Until recently, most studies concluded that dogs were not capable of imitating human models. However there were some studies that indicated dogs made good use of information derived

from us for their own benefit, for example finding the location of hidden food or the best route to reach it. Some years had to elapse before a convincing study on dogs' ability to imitate was published.

The first landmark scientific study of a dog's imitative skills was published in 2006. Researchers from the Ethology Department at the University of Budapest studied the abilities of dogs to replicate the actions of a human model (Topál et al., 2006). The dog in question was named Philip, a 4-year-old Belgian Shepherd Tervuren who worked as an assistance dog.

The results of the study clearly showed that Philip's imitative skills were very strong. In fact, after undergoing training following a protocol very similar to the one described later in this book, Philip was able to replicate the actions of a human demonstrator after observing him.

Was Philip a superdog? Would other dogs be able to do this as well? Would my dogs be capable of doing the same things? I had many questions, so filled with even more curiosity after my research, I decided to put to the test the imitation skills of India, my second Czechoslovakian Wolfdog, by following the protocol described in the study with Philip.

India, like Siria, easily succumbed to my enthusiasm and willingly participated in my many experiments, especially when I offered her some treats in exchange for her cooperation. Excited by the idea of practicing a new game with my dog, I went over the protocol published in the article to test the hypothesis that my dog could learn to perform a behavior by observing and then imitating me doing it. Once I understood what I had to do, I cut meat in convenient sizes to use as a reinforcer and headed to the training field by car. I think that India guessed that I had the intention of proposing an amusing activity, because on the route she was restless, as though she could not wait to start. Finally, we got there and started our adventure! The results we achieved I will share with you in the remainder of the book, but first let's look at the theory and concepts relating to social learning.

2
Social Learning—
An Overview

Social learning in animals occurs when other individuals have a direct influence on an animal's acquisition of a new skill or behavior. This means that, in certain instances, animals can acquire new information or new behaviors through observing the actions of other individuals of the same species or other species that an individual comes in contact with. This stands in contrast to individual non-associative learning based on exposure to a stimulus (e.g., habituation) and to associative learning, by means of connecting various stimuli through classical conditioning or the trial and error attempts typical of operant conditioning that many dog trainers use to teach new behaviors.

Imagine the case of an animal who needs to learn what types of fruits are edible. The animal can adopt the strategy of observing the behavior of other individuals (social learning), or alternatively he can adopt a trial and error strategy, tasting different types of fruits until he finds out which ones can be consumed safely. Doubtless the latter strategy involves significant risks, which helps to illustrate the advantage of social learning over individual learning in that fewer negative consequences are experienced (Zentall, 2004). By observing other members of their social group, individuals can learn the location of important resources like food and water and the techniques to obtain them. They can also learn to recognize predators and other hazards.

In the past, comparative psychologists did not pay much attention to the social learning aspect of animal behavior, the reason being that until recently there was a prevailing opinion that learning through imitation in non-human animals did not exist or was rare. However, through their research, some ethologists have revealed cases of social learning and social influence in a variety of species. Thus, for instance, dolphins seem to amuse themselves by copying the movements of seals, turtles and penguins (Tayler and Saayman, 1973), Indian blackbirds imitate the vocalizations of primates (Tenaza, 1976), and some studies show that chimpanzees are able to replicate human actions (Hayes and Hayes, 1952).

Those species which live in social groups should be more inclined to learn socially. In fact, the transmission of information from one animal to another is much more likely if the animals are in close contact with each other. Other factors that should favor social learning are the existence of parental care, which facilitates the transfer of information from parents to their offspring, and the inclination to explore and to play. When both are present, they increase the opportunities for innovations and discoveries to be passed on socially. Most wild canines (wolves, coyotes, etc.) share these features, but to date there are only limited studies on social learning among them in the wild.

With regard to captive wolves, there is some anecdotal evidence. Wolves locked up in cages have shown an ability to open them after observing their human curators perform the same operation (Frank, 1980).

Unfortunately, before 2000 only a few studies were published about social learning in dogs and they only dealt with learning from other dogs (conspecifics). In one of them, researchers proved that puppies in training to be drug detection dogs learned the necessary skills faster if they were allowed to observe their mothers working (Slabbert and Rasa, 1997).

More recent research has begun to shed light on the dog's social learning skills as they relate to being in contact with humans. The inspiration for this research line originated from a series of studies that compared the behavior of dogs with that of wolves. These two species, despite their phylogenetic relatedness, evolved in different ecological niches. The one major difference between them is that dogs evolved in close contact with humans while wolves did not. Once environmental factors and learning history are controlled for, it can be shown that many of the remaining differences between the two species are due to domestication, which is precisely the process through which the ancestral wolves evolved into dogs.

Some years ago in the Ethology Department of the University of Budapest, where I currently work, researchers carried out a series of studies aimed at examining the behavioral differences between dogs and wolves that were raised in the same environment. The wolf and dog puppies were brought up in the homes of volunteer students and researchers. In one of the tests, researchers presented the animals a problem solving task that had the appearance of a mental stimulation game. The test was designed so that both the dogs and the wolves had to learn by themselves, through trial and error, how to gain access to a tasty treat hidden within an object. Once they had learned to solve the problem, the same subjects were confronted with a variation of the task that was impossible to solve, since access to the food had been deliberately blocked. In the first situation, when the food was accessible, wolves and dogs gained access to the food in comparable times. However, when they faced the insolvable task, there was a significant difference in their behavior: the wolves kept on trying to sort out the problem by themselves; the dogs turned and looked in the direction of their owners as if they were asking for help (Miklósi et al., 2003).

It appears to be the case that this predisposition to look at humans is a characteristic that paved the way to the establishment of the special relationship we share with our dogs. In fact, visual contact is considered to be the starting point of communication. For humans, meaningful visual observation preceded the development of verbal language. It is therefore one of the simplest and most direct forms of communication available. For instance, think of the visual contact between a mother and her child, or the way that we focus our attention on a person's face when we are about to start a conversation. Thus the predisposition of dogs to look at humans, most likely a result of domestication, may have enabled them to establish a strong communication channel with us and may have contributed to rendering our relationship with them so special.

Researchers have also tried to determine if dogs can use the actions of humans as a source of information to solve problems or gain resources. A famous experiment by Pongrácz and others studied the behavior of dogs who were placed behind a V-shaped fence with a highly desirable food or a toy placed on the other side. In this situation, it was found that dogs took a considerable amount of time to learn individually that, in order to reach the object, it was necessary to circumvent the fence. However, when a human demonstrated the detour, the dogs quickly copied what the person did and reached the target within a short time. What was even more surprising was that dogs tended to keep applying the socially learned solution even if another shortcut in the fence was provided that would allow them to reach the object in a more direct and faster way (Pongrácz et al., 2003).

These studies suggest that dogs are predisposed to learn socially from humans and that information acquired through the social learning pathway becomes more ingrained than what is learned through trial and error.

Origin and evolution of social cognitive skills in dogs

People and dogs have been living together for a long time. This coexistence has yielded mutual benefits from the time that some wolves, the ancestors of dogs, discovered human garbage could provide a steady supply of food. These wolves / early dogs probably also provided a service to people in that they kept human settlements clean and intruders away. As the interaction between the two species evolved, people started to breed dogs for specific functions (fighting, guarding, hunting, herding), selecting for those characteristics that were useful for those specific tasks.

While there are many differences between them, humans and wolves organize themselves in social groups and it is possible that this affinity contributed to the evolution of the coexistence between dogs and humans. It is undeniable now that human society is, in almost all cases, the natural environment for dogs. They share our cities and our farms, they find shelter in our houses, and in some cases they even sleep in our beds. Since the time the dog was first domesticated, humans and dogs have shared the same ecological niche (human settlements or the surroundings of human social groups). It is probable that by sharing the same ecological niche, dogs and humans have experienced what is known as convergent evolution, a process that led both species to adopt similar cognitive and behavioral solutions to common challenges (Miklósi and Topál, 2013). By sharing the same social environment, both species developed behavioral traits to carry out some of the same functions and learned to communicate with one another.

According to recent studies, the evolution of dogs alongside humans allowed them to develop specific skills to interpret our communication signals (Hare et al., 2002). For example, experimental studies have revealed that dogs can analyze us skilfullly and understand us when we point at objects (Lakatos et al., 2012). This is not surprising, because those skills constituted an undeniable advantage for dogs who shared our ecological niche. Recent studies have also revealed that dogs are able to interpret our emotions based on our facial expressions.

It now seems clear that dogs have evolved cognitive skills to observe and understand humans that were advantageous in their ecological niche.

Putting a dog's communication skills to the test

A simple experiment will suffice to demonstrate the closeness of a dog's communicative behavior to ours.

Children learn to express themselves with gestures before learning to speak. Thus when they want something, they look and point at the object, swinging their gaze back and forth from the object to the adult. With the game I am about to explain, you will be able to test whether your dog communicates with you in a way similar to the way a child does with an adult.

You will need help from a friend to carry out this experiment. Instruct your friend to hold an object which is particularly desirable to the dog, for instance his/her favorite toy or a treat. Tell your friend to show the object to the dog while you are in another room, then to place it out of the dog's reach, for instance on an upper shelf, but allowing him/her to see the object in its new location. Then tell your friend to go out of the room as you enter. Observe your dog's behavior. It is very likely that, after greeting you, she will try to make you aware of the new location of the object she wants. She will do it very much the way a child would. She will approach the unreachable object and then begin alternating her gaze between your eyes and the object. If your friend did not reveal the new hiding place to you, the game can be made more interesting by measuring the time until the dog indicates the location of her treasure to you.

This simple game is a wonderful way to witness that dogs have developed great communicative skills vis-à-vis humans and also cognitive capabilities comparable in many situations to those exhibited by young children.

Social learning

Just like individual learning, social learning involves a wide range of learning processes. Before we analyze them one by one, a distinction needs to be made between social incentive and social learning (Galef, 1988). Social incentive occurs when the behavioral response is already present in the repertoire of an animal, but he performs it after observing the same behavior performed by another. In other words, it is a phenomenon where the observation of a behavior increases the probability that the observer will perform the same behavior, which is already part of his behavior repertoire. By contrast, social learning involves performing a behavior which the observer did not previously know or involves acquiring some new piece of information.

Some researchers (Withen and Ham, 1992) draw a similar distinction between (1) social learning, where the observer learns from the model some component of the behavior, and (2) social influence, where the behavior of the observer is influenced by the model, but without the observer learning any specific behavioral component.

Imitation

Imitation is a learning process that belongs within the range of behaviors associated with social learning. Despite the fact that in common language imitation gets somewhat bad press, as it is linked to shallow and cheap copying of behavior, in science it is considered a "special ability" that involves complex cognitive skills. Unfortunately there is no agreement among scientists on its definition and therefore there is also no agreement on what species possess the ability to imitate.

Imitation has been defined in many ways. Edward Thorndike, the famous psychologist, was the first one (in 1898) to propose an operative definition of imitation: "learning to do an act from seeing it done." Withen and Ham (1992) define imitation as "the learning of some components of a behavior through the observation of another animal."

Imitation can be broken down into two stages:

1. Observation
2. Replication of the observed behavior

The main cognitive variables involved are:

1. Motivation
2. Attention
3. Memorization
4. Replication

Let us analyze the cognitive variables briefly one by one:

1. Motivation: This is the combination of factors responsible for the initiation, maintenance and cessation of a behavior. With regard to social learning, the dog must be motivated by the desire to observe and subsequently replicate a behavior. Regardless of the technique used, it is important to check that the reinforcers being used will motivate the dog sufficiently.

This means you will have to find out whether your dog prefers playing, food or a form of social gratification (e.g., enthusiastic compliments and cuddles). Use the reinforcer which is most appropriate for each occasion.

2. Attention: A dog must be able to carefully observe the behavior of the handler before being able to replicate it. In other words, the dog must be able to direct his attention to those aspects of the observed phenomenon that he considers relevant.

In this sense, when you teach the imitation rule to your dogs, and when you teach them new behaviors making use of the Do As I Do protocol, it is important that the demonstration of the action the dog is required to copy is sufficiently emphasized and salient so that your dog will be able to understand which parts of the different actions you perform are of relevance to the behavior you are teaching him.

3. Memorization: The dog must be able to remember and subsequently recover the information related to the behavior observed from the model. In the Do As I Do protocol, the demonstration and the dog's performance are not simultaneous, even if they are quite close in time: the dog should remember the behavior we have performed at least until we give the cue "Do it!" In other words, the dog's behavior should not be simultaneous with the model's demonstration and, therefore, it requires some memory skills. In a recently published study, we have discovered that memorization by dogs of human actions can take place over longer time periods than previously thought (Fugazza and Miklósi, 2013).

4. Replication: The behavior the subject is learning must be similar to the one that has been performed by the model. Regarding dogs' imitative abilities, they have been defined as **functional imitation** (Topál et al., 2006). That means the dog can reach the same goal that was reached by the human demonstrator and, given the differences in their species-specific physical and behavioral repertoire, perform a similar action (e.g., if the human picks up an object using his hand, the dog will use his mouth).

On a cognitive level, all four of these variables must be present to define the behavioral correspondence as imitation.

Other social learning processes

As mentioned above, social learning has a wide range of learning processes and imitation is only one of them. Experts have identified other mechanisms beyond imitation which can be responsible for behavioral similarity among individuals. The following will examine some of these processes that can be responsible for behavioral similarity that can be exploited in dog training.

Response facilitation: This consists of the observation and decoding of a behavior which is already part of the behavioral repertoire of the observer, who then selects and executes a motor response corresponding to it. Thus there is no learning of a new behavior. Observers, however, must be able to sort out a correspondence between the observed behaviors and those they offer.

Contagion: This is an unconditioned mechanism in which the model's action elicits the observer's instinctual response. The best example is yawning—we know that humans are stimulated to yawn when they see somebody else doing it. In fact, it appears that yawning is also contagious between humans and dogs. With regard to contagious behavior among dogs, other known examples are barking simultaneously or howling (for instance, how dogs will vocalize in response to an ambulance siren).

Stimulus enhancement and local enhancement: These are the increased attention of the observer toward the object manipulated by the demonstrator (or the location where he acts). This increased attention, as a consequence, increases the probability of performing similar behaviors, because the observer focuses on a certain object or location after seeing the model interacting with that object or aiming at the referred location. Therefore, through these processes, dogs can learn socially with what object or what part of an object to interact, but not what action to perform on it.

Goal emulation: Through goal emulation the observer learns socially what the goal to be achieved is but does not learn socially what actions are needed to achieve it. This learning process is usually considered different from imitation because if imitation occurs, the observer also copies the body movements.

In summary, many researchers suggest that there is a qualitative difference between imitation and these other phenomena. The difference regards a set of distinctive features such as the correspondence of body movements and the novelty, or lack thereof, of the behavior offered by the learner. Thus it can be concluded that in order to label a learning process as "imitation," it is necessary that the behavior of the observer contains a novel component.

3

The Do As I Do
Training Protocol

The Do As I Do protocol consists of two phases. Both of them are necessary for dogs to learn the imitation rule and to empower us to utilize the imitation rule to teach new behaviors. The dog needs to already know six different behaviors that will be used during the two stages of the protocol. After completing both phases, it will be possible to teach the dog brand new behaviors relying on the dog's imitation skills.

Preliminary training

Before starting with the Do As I Do protocol, it is necessary that you teach (or strengthen) six different behaviors, three of which must be under verbal cue. These behaviors can be taught with traditional associative techniques (operant or classical conditioning). A human must also be able to perform and demonstrate the behaviors, so choose something that you can do.

Keep doing the preliminary training until you can verify that at least three behaviors with their respective verbal cues can be performed in random order. In my case, I chose three different behaviors well known to India: lying down, twisting (i.e., spinning around her body axis) and climbing onto an agility table. Your goal is to have the dog know each verbal cue and the behavior it indicates, which in my case meant that India knew the cues for the lie down, the twist and the table behaviors without hesitation.

Avoid making gestures

An important warning is needed at this point. Sometimes we are convinced that our dogs perform a chosen behavior because we have given a verbal cue. However, after analyzing both the dog's and the handler's behavior, you might notice that the dog only sits down when the handler has gestured by hand or has approached the dog and slightly leaned his body toward him. This indicates that stimulus control is not in the words "Sit down," but in a given gesture. If you use a gesture, the verbal cue must come first, as you will learn below.

In truth, when we only rely on gestural communication, we induce dogs to follow, and hence, there is no guarantee that they will acquire a mental representation of the behavior we are asking them to perform. It is comparable to a situation where you are driving to your destination guided by GPS. You will probably not be able to give clear directions to another driver because, while following the GPS indications, you have not formed a "mental map" of the route.

Similarly, for the dog trying to learn the imitation rule in the Do As I Do protocol (that is, "Do it!" means "copy!"), the lack of a mental representation of the behavior will make it harder for the dog to learn the imitation rule in the first training phase. For instance, if a dog performs the behavior mechanically only because you induce him to do it with your gestures (by using your hand as a target), the dog will lack a mental representation because he has no need to acquire it in order to perform the behavior. It is enough for him to mechanically follow the hand inducing gesture and perform the behavior as a mere consequence of the gesture. The absence of a mental representation will make it more difficult for the dog to learn that there is a correspondence between the handler's demonstration and the behavior he is required to perform. Conversely, when a dog has an idea (i.e., a mental representation) of the behavior involved, it will be much easier for him to learn that there is a similarity between the behavior he knows and that modeled by the handler.

Strengthening verbal cues

How do you teach dogs to sit when you give the cue "Sit" without resorting to any inducing gestures? For the dog to learn the value of the word as a cue, *you have to pronounce it right before you give a gestural cue.* You should never give the old gesture at the *same time* as a word that you choose to establish as a new cue. The reason is that if the old gesture and the new verbal cue are given simultaneously, the dog will focus on the gesture he already knows. This induces the behavior mechanically and does not require learning the new word. However, if you give the new verbal cue word beforehand, even if at first the dog may not know what you want him to do, following it later with the gestural cue will provide the dog guidance. In this way, after some repetitions, the dog will associate the new verbal cue with the known gesture that induced the behavior.

For example, imagine that you want to associate a new verbal cue, "Table" with the behavior of getting on to an agility table. For this purpose the correct sequence would be as follows:

- Say the word "Table" without providing any simultaneous gestural indication.
- After half a second, provide the known gestural cue that the dog already knows means "go get on the table."
- Reinforce the dog for performing the correct behavior.

This type of conditioning is based on the principles of associative learning: an association between the word and the gesture emerges because the former always comes before the latter. Therefore it becomes a reliable predictor that allows the dog to know that if he performs the behavior, you will reward his efforts.

Granted this preliminary training does not differ from traditional training techniques. You can skip this review phase of the protocol if you are positive that your dog has already mastered the three behaviors and their corresponding cues (discriminative stimuli).

Do As I Do Phase One: Learning the imitation rule

The aim of the first phase of the protocol described in the following paragraphs is to teach the **imitation rule** to the dog. This involves the dog learning that the cue "Do it!" means "copy the behavior I have just demonstrated" no matter what it is.

- Choose three behaviors for your dog to master. They should already be under stimulus control, preferably a verbal cue.

- Remember that you must choose behaviors that the dog can perform and demonstrate.

- Practice the three behaviors to strengthen the dog's ability to do them on cue.

- Then, stand in front of the dog and ask him to "Stay" or use some other cue that will hold the dog in position (standing, sitting or lying).

- Demonstrate one of the three behaviors that you have decided to use during this first phase of the protocol.

- Return and stand in front of your dog again and use the new cue "Do it!" followed by the specific cue he already knows for the behavior you have just demonstrated (e.g., "Table").

In sum, the sequence consists of the following five steps:

1. Ask the dog to "Stay" and then demonstrate the behavior.
2. Give the new cue: "Do it!"
3. Give the old cue: "Table," for instance.
4. Your dog offers the behavior.
5. You reward the dog for doing so.

Practice with the three behaviors that you have chosen for this first phase. Ask your dog to do only one single behavior at a time and choose it randomly. Do not work for longer than six trials in each session to prevent the dog from getting tired.

Mastering the "Do it!" cue, fading the old cue

While I was working with India on this new game, after a few training sessions, I noticed that after I demonstrated what I wanted her to do, she started to offer the behavior as soon as I gave the verbal cue "Do it!" without waiting for the old cue. This meant that India was beginning to learn the imitation rule.

I was thrilled and India seemed very happy! I rewarded her for copying my behavior immediately after my "Do it!" cue with a jackpot consisting of a tasty handful of treats and put an end to the working session in the most positive way possible: playing with her in the training field, a game she adored. I was pleasantly surprised by her learning skills as I began to experience personally the innate tendency of dogs to learn socially from humans.

As you work with your own dog on this protocol, at some point your dog will also likely start offering the requested behavior right after you have given the "Do it!" cue and before you have the chance to give the old cue as India did. This is the point in the process that indicates that your dog is starting to learn the rules of the game!

Once you reach this stage in your training, you will no longer need the old cue and the sequence will proceed as follows:

1. Demonstrate the behavior.
2. Give the new cue: "Do it!"
3. Your dog performs the behavior.
4. Reward the dog for doing so.

Note that at this point you are still working with behaviors that your dog had previously learned to perform under stimulus control.

Important rules to follow during the training

The dog has now started to learn that "Do it!" means "replicate the behavior I just did." In order to let him master the
rule and to prevent him from using associative learning
instead, it is important to make sure the dog is not being
prompted by some discriminative stimuli. It is critical that the
dog relies only on the demonstration of the action, without
the aid of cues, gestures or other stimuli.

One thing is to take care that you are not inadvertently
giving other cues to your dog that he is reacting to. In fact,
it is not unusual for this to occur. You may find without real-
izing it that at the same time you give the "Do it!" cue, you
move your head or arm slightly or you look at the object that
you want your dog to approach. These inadvertent signals

provide an opportunity for the dog to react to them rather than to focus on the demonstration. This can result in him being cued by the gesture rather than learning to copy the demonstration. This in turn impedes learning of the imitation rule. To learn not to give subtle inadvertent signals (something which may be much more difficult than it would appear at first glance), you should record your training sessions and analyze them later on, trying to detect any inadvertent signals on your part. Another option is to ask a helper to observe the training sessions and provide feedback.

Remember also that in each of the training sessions you should perform the three different behaviors in random order. However, avoid asking for any given behavior more than twice in a row because, if you do, you will increase the probability that the dog offers you the specific behavior not because it matches your previous demonstration, but *because you have reinforced it twice in a row*. Keep in mind that the aim at this stage is to teach dogs that they should rely on your demonstration to perform an action that matches it, so that they will learn that "Do it!" means "copy!"

During your training sessions, avoid asking for the behaviors always in the same order. For instance, you should not always start with the same behavior. Otherwise, the dog may learn the sequence by heart rather than paying attention to the demonstration.

All the objects (table, chair, toy, etc.) that you will be using for the different behaviors must be present during the entire training session. This means that dogs should be free to perform a different behavior than the one you are demonstrating. If they do, they will not receive any reinforcement for doing so.

Try to maintain the attention of the dog during the demonstration using some type of communication, for instance through visual contact. In fact, the importance of this factor has been proven in studies about social learning. For example, the researchers who set up the V-shaped fence problem mentioned earlier also found that the dog's performance was improved when the human model maintained a communicative context with the dog. When there was no sustained communication between the dog and the human model, the dog was much slower to or could not accomplish the task (Pongrácz et al., 2001, 2003, 2005).

With regard to behaviors involving interaction with an object (such as touching a chair with the hand), it is useful to look at the object, as this will help the dog to focus on it and understand the interaction. In summary, maintaining a communicative context is a crucial requirement to put the Do As I Do training protocol into practice.

Four golden rules

These four golden rules should be followed during Do As I Do training (or any other training technique one relies upon).

1. Working sessions must be kept SHORT

Each training session must amount to what is a fun game for your dog to be played in your company. If the dog becomes exhausted, his motivation can decrease and he can be less willing to cooperate with what you are trying to accomplish in the next training session. For this reason, it is important to close the training session before the dog becomes tired, when he is still willing to work (i.e., willing to have fun) with you.

Remember that training sessions should be a fun, playful activity for your dog. This does not mean that you should not work hard to get the training right; it just means that you should be diligent about making it fun for you and especially for your dog. If you respect this rule, you will see that in the next session the dog's motivation will likely increase.

Keep in mind also that this training technique is not merely based on the establishment of associations between stimuli and responses. It requires the dog to use his cognitive social skills. The dog will likely get tired relatively quickly because this implies much concentration. A good strategy to ensure that you do not overextend the training session out of enthusiasm is to count the treats you are delivering to the dog. But do not forget to offer a jackpot when you come across a particularly good response!

On average a six-trial session is sufficient and after the training it is ideal to provide the dog a place to relax body and mind.

2. Pause immediately if you detect signs of STRESS in the dog

Learning something new is always a stressful mental challenge. In any training situation, it is likely that the dog will not understand the purpose of the game at the beginning. If you notice at any point that the stress level is excessive, it is better to stop the training session at once and only resume it after the dog has rested and is calmer. In fact, excessive amounts of stress are not only bad for your dog but also compromise his ability to learn.

3. Always end the training session with a SUCCESS from the dog (and for you!)

If your dog fails with a difficult exercise, do not set him up for failure again and again. The right thing to do is to simplify the exercise a bit and end the working session on a high note.

4. Let your dog take a BREAK

Working sessions must be kept short to be effective for learning. Asking for six consecutive trials represents a significant mental effort and it is more than enough for most dogs. For some dogs this length may even be excessive.

By stopping before the dog gets tired, learning will be much more effective and the dog will not lose the motivation to work with you. Sometimes the enthusiasm for what you are doing or the attempt to obtain immediate results can lead you to prolong the working sessions too much. Rather than waiting for your dog to be tired or stressed, it is good practice to end the session while your dog is still willing to work. After a training session it is of the utmost importance to grant your dog a break.

Contrary to how it may seem, what you have your dog do during a break is crucial. In the courses I teach, I have seen some students making use of the pause to practice other activities with their dogs: agility, ball chasing, etc. Remember that the pause has to be truly that, a *break!* Instead of pressing a dog to engage in other activities during a break, let them rest body and mind. The best thing to do is to offer some rest in a quiet area. In this way your dog will soon be ready to play and to learn at your side again. Moreover, sleeping may contribute to consolidate the dog's memory of the lessons learned in the training session.

Do As I Do Phase Two: Generalizing the imitation rule

Before moving on to Phase Two, your dog should be replicating the first three behaviors that you chose to work on. Instead of waiting for the known cue attached to the behavior, the dog should now be reacting as soon as the "Do it!" cue is given.

Once the dog reaches a high success rate imitating three known behaviors immediately after being given the "Do it!" cue, it is time to take a step further and introduce three other known behaviors. While these behaviors are known by the dog, make sure you have not yet used them in the context of the Do As I Do protocol. Therefore, at this point of the training plan, you will be working with six different known behaviors, three of which were used in Phase 1 and three that were not but are familiar to the dog. The goal of this stage is for the dog to **generalize** the imitation rule to the three other known behaviors that you have not worked on yet in the Do As I Do context.

During this second stage the same rules that applied during the previous stage still prevail. As you will remember, the aim is to ensure that the dog makes a choice based solely on the demonstration performed by the human model without relying on prompts or other discriminative stimuli inadvertently provided. Hence, once more I remind you that it is good practice to record the training sessions in order to track any mistakes (e.g., providing any inadvertent signals to the dog) and correct them.

The critical point in your efforts to generalize the imitation rule is to pick one of the three behaviors you have not worked on yet. Remember in Phase One that you began by using the "Do it!" cue followed immediately after by the verbal cue already known by the dog. Now, instead of also using the known verbal cue, just use the "Do it!" cue. If the dog really understands that "Do it!" means to do what the handler has just done, then the dog has indeed generalized the imitation rule. If your dog comes across any difficulties in replicating any of those behaviors, you can resort to the old cue attached to that behavior after the "Do it!" signal, as we did at the beginning of the first stage of the protocol. Sometimes difficulties may arise due to the anatomic differences between humans and dogs. Thus the divergence in the way we carry out certain behaviors may make it harder for the dog to find the right match for the behavior demonstrated.

Changing human models

To further strengthen your dog's ability to imitate success-fully, I recommend at the end of this phase that you gener-alize the imitation rule using a different person to perform the demonstration and to give the "Do it!" command. In the research project mentioned early in the book, in order to verify Philip's imitation skills, researchers substituted the regular trainer with other human models. Philip proved that his learning and generalization of the imitation rule was sufficiently strong to succeed despite the presence of new people doing the demonstration.

The introduction of a new handler/model can be useful in order to improve the generalization of the imitation rule. Therefore, if you have the chance, once you have com-pleted the first two stages of the protocol, ask a friend to work with your dog using the same technique. The new han-dler should do exactly the same things that you have been doing. My advice is that you allow the new trainer to observe you working with your dog before trying him/herself. It will be much easier for your dog if the new trainer works in a similar way, particularly during the first sessions.

Changing human models also proves with a greater degree of certainty that the dog is actually imitating and not just picking a few cues inadvertently emitted by the owner.

Now it is time to try to teach your dog entirely new behaviors using the Do As I Do protocol!

4

Do As I Do—Training New Behaviors

Working with India

As I worked with my dog India, I was surprised by the results achieved. It was not only that India understood the rules of the game perfectly but that she also adored it. The enthusiasm she showed while I was getting ready for a training session kept increasing, and India was not only eager, she kept getting better all the time. Encouraged by the results I was obtaining with India and her passion for this new game, I dared to go a step further and made the decision to teach a *completely new behavior* relying on the new method.

I reflected on it for two days before picking a new behavior, which consisted of circling an object, more specifically a cone. This was a brand new behavior for India, so I did not know if it would be too difficult, but I had to give it a try. Once again, armed with a video camera and treats, I set the stage.

I placed the cone a couple of meters away from me in the agility field where we usually work. In the meantime, India was so enthusiastic that she kept on jumping on me in an attempt to lick my mouth and also tried to steal some treats from my pouch.

The procedure I used was similar to that applied in the course of previous sessions. I asked India to sit and stay while observing my demonstration. The only difference was that on this occasion the behavior I demonstrated was completely unknown to her. I walked away from her and circled the cone. Then, after reaching my initial position, I gave India the "Do it!" cue and, without hesitating, she trotted up to the cone and circled it before coming back while she wagged her tail and asked for a treat.

Brava, India!

She had understood it in the blink of an eye!

I was radiant; it worked!

At this point I could conclude that India indeed had learned a new behavior. Unless I always wanted to demonstrate it, however, I had to now put it under stimulus control (i.e., attach a new cue to the behavior), making use of traditional training techniques. After a few minutes I could say the word "Cone," and India would proudly trot toward the object and circle it before coming back.

Now let's turn to what you need to do to teach new behaviors!

How to teach new behaviors

After the dog has learned the imitation rule (by working on the set of three known behaviors during the first stage of the protocol) and generalized it (by working on the set of six known behaviors, the three used in Phase One plus the three added in Phase Two, during the second stage of the protocol), you can use the Do As I Do method for teaching new behaviors to your dog.

Just like with the progression from Phase One to Phase Two, progress to new behaviors only if the results achieved in the second phase are good. This means that you should only teach new behaviors through imitation after your dog has shown he makes no or few mistakes in imitating the six known behaviors.

By now you have reached the point that your dog knows that "Do it!" means "reproduce the behavior I have just performed." With this background it should not be difficult to teach new behaviors, and the process for it is always the same:

- Ask your dog to stay still and to observe you.
- Demonstrate the new behavior.
- Return to the initial position.
- Give the cue "Do it," whose meaning is now known by the dog.
- If the dog offers the right behavior, reward the dog. Otherwise, start over from the beginning, running the demonstration once more.

In this way the dog will learn a new behavior. However, how should we define a new behavior? I suggest that "new" can consist of the application of an action which is known to the dog in a different context or with regard to a new object. For example, if the dog knows how to touch a target with the paw, you can teach him to turn on the lights by pressing the switch with his paw. Touching an object with the paw is a known action, but now the dog has to touch a new object, the switch. Therefore it is a new behavior for our purposes.

It could also consist of a completely new behavior, for example, like circling the cone, where not only the object but also the action was unknown to India.

Try to pay attention and carefully assess which are the difficult and novel elements so that you can simplify the training process as much as possible and set your dog up for success.

Putting the new behavior under stimulus control

Now we come back full circle. After some repetitions to see if the dog can correctly imitate the behavior, it will be possible to put the new behavior under a verbal cue so that you will not need to demonstrate the behavior yourself every time you want your dog to do it. The first thing you need to do is to introduce a new cue between the demonstration and the cue which is already known ("Do it," in this case). Thus the appropriate order is:

- Demonstration.
- New cue (for instance, "Touch").
- Old cue ("Do it!").
- Your dog offers the behavior.
- Reinforcement.

After a few repetitions, you will be able to skip the demonstration of the behavior as well as the attached old cue ("Do it!"). So now the process will be:

- New cue (for instance, "Touch").
- Your dog offers the behavior.
- Reinforcement.

In a nutshell, only the new cue and the new behavior will finally remain.

Spreading the word

I was starting to think that, based on what India had done, dogs' imitation skills could be used to teach them new behaviors. Although my test was limited to a single case and I needed to verify the results with other subjects, it certainly looked like a promising start! Meanwhile summer arrived with its heat and I was forced to cut the duration of the training sessions drastically, limiting them to a few minutes at dawn.

Later in the year, I scheduled the first seminar about social learning as a training technique at my dog training center, making it clear to the prospective students that it was still a work in progress but that I was eager to teach other owners and their dogs what I had learned. This would provide me the opportunity to apply this technique to teach new behaviors to dogs other than my own.

Every dog is special for its owner, but I did not think that India was unique with regard to her imitation skills. And, I knew that in order to conclude with certainty that this technique could be applied to teach new behaviors, evidence based on working with one dog was not good enough. The theory that the imitation rule could be used to train new behaviors needed to be verified with several experimental subjects.

The seminar participants (both human and canine) had curiosity and enthusiasm, the right combination I needed. I already knew some of them from previous courses: Vudu, a French Bulldog who was incredibly good in agility; Lilly, a little and adorable pain in the neck disguised as a Jack Russell Terrier; a second but different Lilly who was a very shy Yorkshire Terrier; Clio, a very sweet bitch of an uncertain breed; and Suri, a restless Border Collie cross. The seminar also gave me the chance to make some new friends like Africa, a beautiful and thoughtful female Belgian Shepherd Groenendael; Funky and Tosca, both of them gray and very clever German Shepherds; and Lulú an Italian wolf dog.

With them and their determined owners we put into practice the protocol I had developed to teach the imitation rule to the dogs. Then, we applied the technique to teach them new behaviors. The results achieved were consistent with the outcomes I had achieved with India.

We also learned that there were benefits beyond dogs learning to imitate their handlers. As a by-product of the training, some problem behaviors improved. Suri learned to focus on her owner, conquering the restlessness that had seemed to be an insurmountable barrier. Lilly the Yorkshire Terrier's shyness faded away, leaving in place an immense cheerfulness. Funky, who was resigned not to ever take the initiative, blossomed thanks to the patience and persistence of her owner, and both of them started enjoying the advantages of a visibly improved relationship.

In summary, all of them found that this protocol, which revolved around an entertaining game, was not only useful to teach new behaviors. It also opened the door to an improved relationship between dogs and humans. The reason could be that this type of learning is based on social cognitive skills, allowing both dogs and humans to achieve a deep and reciprocal level of understanding. That was precisely what happened to me and India: after this experience we could understand each other on the fly. Apparently this technique allows dogs to reach a deeper level of consciousness about themselves, their human companions and their own skills.

Since that first seminar, I have taught numerous groups this fun training technique. I have always found a warm reception from the participants regardless of whether they had two or four legs. The results have also been impressive. Today I apply this technique daily for teaching dogs new behaviors and, of course, the study of dogs' social cognitive skills remains my main goal.

My curiosity to discover the things that dogs can understand, together with my desire to improve dog training techniques so as to allow dogs to use their cognitive skills to the full, led me to work with Professor Ádam Miklósi from the Ethology Department at the University of Budapest. There my research project became a fully fledged Ph.D. project.

Chained behaviors

At the end of the training program with Philip, the first dog who learned to imitate with the Do As I Do protocol, researchers decided to test his ability to replicate sequences of known actions. To test it, a human model performed two actions, one after the other, and then asked Philip to replicate the entire sequence. The behaviors were not new for Philip, but it was the first time that he had been asked to imitate two behaviors in a row.

What was the outcome? While Philip made some errors, he also managed to repeat action sequences of behavior more frequently that would be expected by pure chance. The most frequent error dogs make in this scenario is a bias in favor of the last behavior performed by the human model. The dogs tend to start with the last behavior or they tend to perform only the last behavior. The actual explanation for why this occurs is not completely known yet, but it could be due to the so-called recency effect, a memory bias in favor of the actions last observed.

You can test this with your dog too. If you do so, take into account that the way you place the objects for the chained behaviors can increase or decrease the difficulty of the challenge. Obviously it will be easier if the objects are lined up in such a way that the dog first encounters the object related to the first behavior; next, the one related to the second behavior; and so on. By placing the objects in this way you will maximize the chance that the dog will perform the behavior chain correctly. Once the dog executes the chain smoothly, you will be able to move the objects gradually until you can set them in the position of your choice.

By working with many dogs I have realized that some of them, especially those who are not very confident, can get stuck after offering the first behavior: some of them kept on looking at the owner as if they were asking for further instructions or a bit of help. One of my students, Africa's owner, wanted to teach her dog a behavior sequence consisting of two actions: (1) placing her front paws on a chair and (2) ringing a bell that was hanging on a string. Right after her owner's demonstration, Africa walked to the chair, put her paws on it, and then got stuck in that position while she kept looking at her owner all the time.

How can you overcome this problem? Not rewarding the dog is tantamount to saying that his/her behavior was incorrect. Nevertheless, in Africa's case, at least the first behavioral link was correct. Thus I asked the owner about the techniques she used to teach new behaviors to her dog. She explained to me that she usually rewarded her dog for performing successive approximations to the target behavior, a technique typically known as shaping or "free shaping." This technique had taught Africa to expect constant confirmations in order to learn step by step, by trials and errors, what the final behavior was about.

After analyzing this, we made the decision to have Africa understand that placing her front paws on the chair was the first step to the final behavior. We relied on a bridging stimulus for that purpose, the word "Brava!" By using this word, we were able to mark the instant that Africa placed her paws on the chair but withheld the primary reinforcer until she completed the entire chain. Probably our "Brava!" worked as an encouragement for Africa to go on and perform also the next action of the sequence.

Today, thanks to the careful work of her owner, Africa has become very precise at replicating each link of behavior chains and she adores practicing this game. The owner has also had a great time making up new behaviors for Africa, which she practices with an ever-growing enthusiasm.

Each dog is an individual. Therefore, the way we tackled Africa's problem may not be useful or even appropriate for all other dogs. As a matter of fact, bridging stimuli are unnecessary in many cases.

In general, imitating behavior chains is a difficult task for all dogs. The personality and learning history of each dog deeply influences the ability to learn new behaviors. For this reason, the decision to rely on bridging stimuli or to skip them, to encourage the dog to continue after performing the first action, and to determine how to place the objects he is working with most effectively are not easy choices to make. It is up to you to make the decisions that suit your dog best by taking into account the knowledge you possess about him or her.

Interestingly, in a recent study (Fugazza and Miklósi, 2014) we discovered that action sequences that have a goal (e.g., open a drawer and pick up an item that is inside of it) are more efficiently taught by the Do As I Do method compared to a traditional training method that relies on individual learning.

5

What to Do If...

Here follows some suggestions so that you can know what to do if problems arise in each of the following scenarios.

Favorite behavior

After placing objects at an equal distance from the dog and from you, you demonstrate a behavior and then observe that your dog always performs the same action with just one object regardless of what you demonstrate and ask him to perform. What is the reason for this?

The behavior in question may be the dog's "favorite." This may occur because in the past the behavior has been reinforced more often than the others. Another possibility is that the behavior is self-rewarding, meaning that performing the behavior is intrinsically reinforcing for the dog even in the absence of an external reinforcer.

What can you do? In most cases, it will be enough to place the favorite object a few meters further away than the distance you have practiced with before. That means that the dog will be obliged to incur an extra effort to perform his favorite behavior instead of what you demonstrate. This simple intervention often suffices to restore the balance among the different behaviors involved. However, if the problem persists, another strategy would be to exclude the object in question for a couple of training sessions and then reincorporate it. If you choose the latter solution, be careful when you reintroduce the favorite item: the dog must not see you manipulating the object, because that would promote further interaction through the phenomenon known as stimulus enhancement, as explained earlier in the book. To prevent problems, have the dog removed from the training field and position all the objects back in place before inviting the dog to enter the field again and resuming training.

Poisoned behavior

At the opposite end of the spectrum, some dogs may dislike a given behavior and, for that reason, they might refuse to offer it. In such cases it is always important to ask yourself why this is so. The first thing to consider is whether the dog feels pain when executing the behavior: jumping over an obstacle, lying down or climbing up on a platform are examples of behaviors that may be painful for some dogs if they cause strain in their backs or joints. If you suspect that your dog may have a physical ailment, ask your veterinarian to explore the issue in depth. In the meantime, replace the problematic behavior with a different one that does not tax the dog with a physical effort.

However, if you are positive that the origin of the problem has nothing to do with pain, you can run a specific training session for the behavior in question with traditional techniques before you try again to teach it to the dog using the imitation rule.

The dog anticipates

Once dogs learn the imitation rule, they tend to anticipate and perform a behavior without waiting for the cue "Do it." I experienced this with India when I realized that she sometimes was not waiting for the cue but rather would leap to imitate once she had understood the behavior I was demonstrating. The problem with anticipation is that it can lead to a situation where both the handler and the dog perform the behavior simultaneously. This would jeopardize the dog's attention, a prerequisite to memorizing and replicating new and/or complex behaviors with success.

To offset this risk, work on the Stay behavior in the following way. Ask your dog to stay still in the usual position. Go back a few steps and then return immediately to reward your dog for staying with compliments and food treats. Repeat the sequence once again, but add some more distance. Finally, increase the distance even more until you can demonstrate one of the behaviors with the dog staying put. However, when you come back to the initial position, reinforce the dog for not breaking the stay instead of giving the cue "Do it." This way in a training session you can sometimes reward the dog for the Stay behavior and sometimes give the "Do it!" command instead, so that the dog will never know if he will be rewarded for the Stay behavior or for copying the behavior after the "Do it!" cue.

Why do dogs anticipate? I have asked myself this question many times, but there is no simple answer. I believe there may be two main reasons. On the one hand, we should not forget that dogs belong to a species with strong social tendencies and who have adapted themselves to recognize humans as social companions. This explains why dogs tend to synchronize their behavior to ours.

A second, alternative explanation (which, however, does not exclude the previous one) is that after a certain number of Do As I Do training sessions, the dog learns to recognize the situation: the Stay behavior and the focus on the demonstration make the dog understand that he is playing the imitation game. Hence the cue "Do it!" becomes superfluous for the dog. Anyway, if your dog starts replicating your behavior before the cue, do not reward; recall him/her gently, and practice the Stay behavior as explained above before resuming training.

The dog gets fatigued or stressed

If your dog gets distracted during the working session while you are demonstrating a behavior, you may have worked for too long. Sometimes the signs of stress and fatigue are very subtle, but it is crucial to learn to recognize them on time.

It is also very important to stop training *before* the dog starts signalling fatigue—short sessions promote faster learning and they are the best strategy to ensure that the dog will show an increased motivation level in the next session.

If you have made the error of prolonging the training session to the point where the dog gets distracted, try a very simple exercise for your dog (even a simple "Sit"), reward for it, and end the session.

However, if your dog gets easily distracted and this has nothing to do with fatigue or stress levels, you should practice attention exercises, which are a prerequisite for any form of training and should be taught in all foundation courses. Call the dog's attention using his or her name (or with a sound produced with your tongue), then as soon as the dog looks at your face, mark the behavior with a click or a word of your choice ("Bravo") and reward with food.

Repeat the attention exercise several times, gradually increasing the time you require the dog to maintain eye contact before marking and rewarding the behavior. Despite its simplicity, this exercise allows your dog to increase the degree of concentration toward you and may further improve mutual understanding. Visual contact is crucial, since it forms the communication channel between you and your dog.

New locations/environment

Regardless of the training technique you use, your dog will likely experience difficulties learning new exercises in new places sometimes, even if you work on already trained tasks. Therefore, it is a good idea to generalize the behaviors you are teaching to different locations.

Each time you bring your dog to train in a new location, you should allow him to explore it and its scents before starting any training. The information that your dog will collect through this exploration is crucial for him to be able to concentrate on the exercises you are asking him to perform. In other words, you will not be able to train your dog if he is not at ease with the environment. Moreover, excessive stress levels hinder learning. Therefore, it is likely that an uncomfortable dog will not be able to learn anything.

If the dog keeps feeling uncomfortable after exploring the environment, it is recommended that you change locations and select one where the dog shows he can be relaxed and focus on the exercises you are working on.

Along the same lines, it will be necessary to generalize the objects used for training purposes too. For instance, if you teach a dog to go to a particular chair, you may come across difficulties when you vary the shape, the appearance, the seat material or any other features of the chair. To prevent problems, allow your dog to become familiar with the new object before asking him to perform a behavior.

Distractions

Whenever you work with your dog, you should control the environment so that he has the best chance to learn. This means that he should have the opportunity to concentrate. An environment filled with distractions (like a busy public park) is far from ideal to learn new skills.

It is important to get your dog used to focusing on you even when there are external stimuli competing for his attention. To achieve this, you should start with a quiet environment and increase the level of distractions gradually, always ensuring that the dog succeeds despite the gradual increase in the level of difficulty.

If your dog fails, you should take a step back and go on working with less intrusive distractions so that the dog feels confident, focused and at ease. Only then, gradually increase the level of the distractions.

6

Using Do As I Do as Part of an Overall Training Plan

Do As I Do can play an important role in training dogs, as you have seen. It should be clear by now that it is possible to train dogs using social learning and the training protocol introduced in this book. However, in my opinion, we should not limit ourselves to using one single training method. The major benefits accrue from the combined used of social learning with other techniques.

When is Do As I Do training recommended?

In what situations does the "Do As I Do" training protocol work best? According to the research we have been carrying out, Do As I Do is particularly useful to teach behaviors *involving interaction with objects.* A prime example would be the skills typically taught to dogs who assist people with special needs. This could include simple behaviors like ringing a bell or closing a door, or more complex behaviors such as opening a drawer. You can also probably see how it could be useful in training competitive obedience and agility dogs. It is in such situations that dogs benefit in particular from a human demonstrating the target behavior compared to using only traditional learning pathways like, for instance, those based on individual learning processes.

A possible explanation is that the behaviors involving the use of an object compared to those that are only body movements usually have an objective which is more easily observable and learned socially by the dog, for example grabbing the handle of the drawer and pulling it to open the drawer and gain access to its contents. A second possible explanation rests in that dogs have more limited skills, compared to humans, for actions involving their bodies. For instance, dogs do not have hands, which may result in a limitation of the associated cognitive skills and in turn limit mental representations of the actions by their use, e.g., as would occur when you touch your nose with your hand. A third hypothesis to explain this asymmetry in favor of behaviors revolving around an object rests on the phenomenon known as stimulus enhancement. When an observer sees a model manipulating a certain object, the probability of replicating the same behavior increases because the learner's attention is focused on the object. Since the ability of dogs to imitate different actions with a given object has been demonstrated often, it suggests that they possess skills to select the corresponding motor response that go beyond the stimulus enhancement hypothesis. This finding proves their ability to imitate.

These results are endorsed by research that we have recently concluded that proves the Do As I Do method is more efficient than a training method that relies only on individual learning for training complex actions such as opening a drawer and then picking up an item that was placed inside of it. Moreover, these results are consistent with those already known with regard to human learning. A study carried out by McElreath and others (2005) found that humans tend to rely more on social learning over individual learning as the degree of difficulty of the task is increased.

In addition to its potential as a training tool for reaching behavioral goals of an exclusively practical nature, I believe that social learning can greatly improve the relationship between dogs and their owners. The reason is that these techniques directly connect with the natural inclination of dogs to learn socially from humans. In practice this means that you can resort to Do As I Do regardless of the behavior you want to teach to your dog if your main goal is to stimulate playful activity that can improve the uniquely special bond between the two of you.

Social learning is not always the right choice

While hopefully I have shown that using Do As I Do / imitation can be an effective tool when training dogs, Do As I Do will not always be the right choice. For instance, it is apparent from the examples used in this book that it is much easier for dogs to replicate behaviors that consist of interactions with an object rather than body actions such as spinning or sitting. While social learning could be employed, using classical or operant conditioning methods for object-less behaviors like sitting and spinning would likely be more efficient. Furthermore, not every behavior can be imitated. Some actions that dogs are typically required to learn, like "Come" and "Walk on leash," cannot be taught by the Do As I Do method.

Will dogs really remember our behaviors?

A question that is likely in the mind of many readers is will my dog really remember a behavior learned through imitation over a long period of time? This is an understandable concern of trainers. I believe it has been proven that behavior can be learned with this protocol, but trainers need to be convinced that the dogs have the ability to remember the sample behavior and the capacity to recover that memory at a later time.

The scientific term for the cognitive ability to recover a memory of a demonstrated behavior and imitate it at a later time is called **deferred imitation**. The term is used to describe something considered qualitatively different from those processes in which two similar behaviors from two different individuals occur simultaneously or almost simultaneously. For instance, seeing someone yawning may elicit the same behavior from a dog. Since this is an instinctual reaction, there is no complex cognitive process involved and the second behavior, the copied yawn, is close in time to the initial yawn. While there is no set rule, a minimum 60-second time interval has been deemed sufficient to qualify something as deferred imitation rather than a triggered instinctual behavior like the yawning example.

My colleagues and I were curious about whether dogs have deferred imitation abilities or not. Hence, together with Professor Miklósi (Fugazza and Miklósi, 2013), I ran an experiment to verify whether dogs possess the cognitive skills necessary to memorize the behaviors demonstrated by their owners and to perform them after a given time interval. Our initial goal was to understand if dogs were able to recall the behavior demonstrated after one minute had elapsed from the end of the owner's demonstration.

This study had been done on human children, but it has never been replicated in dogs. Our hypothesis was that dogs were a good candidate to test these skills: they belong to a species that evolved in a complex social environment and where the ability to remember the actions of others might have been advantageous. However, we had no idea what was to come out of the research because one minute seemed to us a really long time interval, compared to the usual interval between demonstration and "Do it!" in a normal Do As I Do training session.

For the study we recruited a group of eight dogs and their owners, all of them full of enthusiasm. Among the dogs there were four Border Collies (Phoebe, Minnie, Bambù and Soley), one Shetland Sheepdog (Emma), a Yorkshire Terrier (Lilly), a mongrel dog (Adila) and my Czechoslovakian Wolfdog, India. All of them had been previously trained with the Do As I Do protocol by their respective owners. Therefore, they knew that "Do it!" meant "copy the behavior I have just demonstrated." In order to test our hypothesis, these dogs now had to learn a new rule: copy a behavior that was demonstrated some length of time before, rather than immediately afterward.

We trained the dogs step by step starting with a five-second delay between the end of the demonstration and the cue "Do it." This interval was progressively lengthened until it was doubled to ten seconds. We experienced moments full of tension and emotions while we waited for the dogs to receive the cue from their owners.

After the first day of work, we realized by observing the videos we made during the training that the dogs kept looking at the object they had to interact with during the whole duration of the interval. Since this could be refreshing the memory (working memory) of the behavior demonstrated by the dog's owner, it was not a valid test of deferred imitation. Therefore we had to come up with a slightly different experimental design to truly understand the memorization abilities of the dogs.

After a few attempts, it was Angela (Phoebe's owner) who came up with the idea of taking the dogs behind a screen while they waited together with their handlers. In that way they could no longer see the objects during the waiting time. Phoebe was perfectly at ease with this procedure and, once a short interval elapsed, Angela invited her to resume the exercise and she successfully imitated the demonstrated behavior.

I decided to adopt this procedure for the tests. In each trial the handler demonstrated a behavior chosen at random while the dog stayed still and observed the demonstration. Then, both the dog and the handler walked behind the screen, where they stayed for a given time. Finally, they came back to the starting position and the handler gave the cue "Do it!"

All teams took part in various tests performed under different conditions. We were impressed by the fact that the dogs were successful in imitating their owners despite the use of increasingly long time intervals, reaching even ten minutes! Furthermore, the dogs were capable of recalling the demonstrated behaviors in those trials where they were exposed to distractions (playing with a ball or doing other exercises) during the time interval.

Our research has shown for the first time that dogs possess the ability to engage in deferred imitation. As a matter of fact, similar results with regard to children have been interpreted as implying that prelinguistic children already exhibit incipient declarative memory skills. Applying these results to everyday life, we can now discern how our furry friends are perfectly capable of remembering the actions that we have performed to open the trash bin or a water tap, even after some time has passed. We just have to decide whether we want to feel annoyed by the mess in the kitchen or marvel at the awesome social cognitive skills of our dogs!

In conclusion

My research on social learning in dogs keeps progressing and I hope to be able to answer some of the many questions that curiosity leads us to ask.

One of the most beautiful traits of science is that something is only valid until we come across data that refutes it. This means that new discoveries have the potential to undermine the old tenets which have governed our knowledge so far. Therefore, the pages which I have written may need to be revised and updated in the future. I will be happy if that is the case because it will mean that our knowledge will have made a step forward!

In order to carry out my research on social learning I need help from six-legged collaborators, that is, from dogs and their owners. If you are interested, check the website www. apprendimentosociale.it/en, where you will find all the information necessary to take part in this adventure.

I also want to thank the dogs (shown below) whose owners allowed them to participate in my seminars. Our findings could not have been validated without their help!

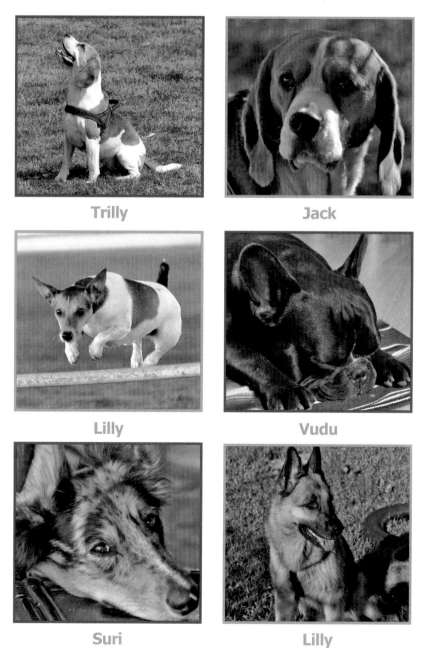

Trilly

Jack

Lilly

Vudu

Suri

Lilly

Bibliography

Braem M.D. & Mills D.S. (2010). "Factors affecting response of dogs to obedience instruction: A field and experimental study." *Applied Animal Behaviour Science* 125:47–55.

Byrne R.W. (1994). "The evolution of intelligence." In Slater P.J.B. and Halliday T.R. (eds.), *Behaviour and Evolution.* Cambridge University Press, Cambridge, pp 223-264.

Cooper J.J. (2003). "Clever hounds: Social cognition in the domestic dog (Canis familiaris)." *Applied Animal Behaviour Science* 81:229–244.

Demant H., Ladewig J., Balsby T.J.S., Dabelsteen T. (2011). "The effect of frequency and duration of training sessions on acquisition and long-term memory in dogs." *Applied Animal Behaviour Science* 133:228-234.

Dorrance R., Zentall T.R. (2001). "Imitative learning in Japanese quail (Coturnix japonica) depends on the motivational state of the observer quail at the time of observation." *Journal of Comparative Psychology* 115:62-67.

Fugazza C. & Miklósi A. (2013). "Deferred imitation and declarative memory in dogs." *Animal Cognition* DOI 10.1007/s10071-013-0656-5.

Fugazza C. & Miklósi A. (2014) "Should old dog trainers learn new tricks? The efficiency of the Do As I Do method and shaping/clicker training method to train dogs." *Applied Animal Behaviour Science* DOI 10.1016/j.applanim.2014.01.009.

Galef B.J. (1988). "Imitation in animals: History, definition, and interpretation of data from the psychological laboratory." In Zentall T.R., Galef B.J. (eds.), *Social Learning: Psychological and Biological Perspectives.* Hillsdale, NJ: Erlbaum pp 3-28.

Galef B.G. & Giraldeau L.A. (2001). "Social influences on foraging in vertebrates: Causal mechanisms and adaptive functions." *Animal Behaviour* 61:3–15.

Hare B., Brown M., Williamson C., Tomasello M. (2002). "The domestication of social cognition in dogs." *Science* 298:1634–1636. DOI: 10.1126/science.1072702.

Hayes K.J. & Hayes C. (1952). "Imitation in a home-raised chimpanzee." *Journal Comp Psychol* 45:450–459.

Huber L., Range F., Voelkl B., Szucsich A., Viranyi Z., Miklósi A. (2009). "The evolution of imitation: What do the capacities of non-human animals tell us about the mechanisms of imitation?" *Philosophical Transactions of the Royal Society* 364, 2299-2309.

Kubinyi E., Pongrácz P., Miklósi A. (2009). "Dogs as a model for studying conspecific and heterospecific social learning." *Journal of Veterinary Behavior* 4:31-41.

Kubinyi E., Topál J., Miklósi A., Csanyi V. (2003). "Dogs (Canis familiaris) learn from their owners via observation in a manipulation task." *Journal of Comparative Psychology* 117:156–165.

Kuczaj S.A. & Yeater D.B. (2006). "Dolphin imitation: Who, what, when and why?" *Aquatic Mammals* 32:413-422, DOI 10.1578/AM.32.4.

Lakatos, G., Gácsi, M., Topál, J., Miklósi, Á. (2012). "Comprehension and utilisation of pointing gestures and gazing in dog–human communication in relatively complex situations." *Animal Cognition* 15:201-213.

Lindsay S.R. (2005). *Handbook of Applied Dog Behavior and Training.* Blackwell Publishing (Vol. 1 and 3).

Madsen E.A. & Persson T. (2012). "Contagious yawning in domestic dog puppies (Canis lupus familaris): The effect of ontogeny and emotional closeness on low-level imitation in dogs." *Animal Cognition* 16:233-240 DOI: 10.1007/s10071-012-0568-9.

McElreath R., Lubellb M., Richersonb P.J., Waring T.M., Baum W., Edsten E. Efferson C., Paciotti, B. (2005). "Applying evolutionary models to the laboratory study of social learning." *Evolution of Human Behavior.* 26, 6:483-508.

Miklósi Á., Kubinyi E., Topál J., Gácsi M., Virányi Z., Csányi V. (2003). "A simple reason for a big difference: Wolves do not look back at humans but dogs do." *Current Biology* 13:763-766.

Miklósi Á. & Soproni K. (2006). "A comparative analysis of animals' understanding of the human pointing gesture." *Animal Cognition* 9:81–93, DOI: 10.1007/s10071-005-0008-1.

Miklósi Á., Topál J., Csányi V. (2007). "Big thoughts in small brains? Dogs as a model for understanding human social cognition." *NeuroReport* 18:467-471.

Miklósi Á. (2007). *Dog Behaviour Evolution and Cognition.* Oxford, Oxford University Press.

Miklósi Á. & Topál J. (2013). "What does it take to become 'best friends'? Evolutionary changes in canine social competence." *Trends in Cognitive Science* 17:287-294. http://dx.doi.org/10.1016/j.tics.2013.04.005.

Miklósi A. (1999). "The ethological analysis of imitation." *Biological Reviews* 74:347-374.

Pongrácz P., Miklósi A., Kubinyi E., Gurobi K., Topál J., Csanyi V. (2001). "Social learning in dogs: The effect of a human demonstrator on the performance of dogs in a detour task." *Animal Behaviour* 62:1109–1117.

Pongrácz P., Miklósi A., Kubinyi E., Topál J., Csanyi V. (2003). "Interaction between individual experience and social learning in dogs." *Animal Behaviour* 65:595–603

Pongrácz P., Miklósi A, Timar-Geng K., Csanyi V. (2003). "Preference for copying unambiguous demonstration in dogs (Canis familiaris)." *Journal of Comparative Psychology* 117:337–343.

Pongrácz P., Miklósi A., Vida V., Csanyi V. (2005). "The pet dog's ability for learning from a human demonstrator in a detour task is independent from breed and age." *Applied Animal Behaviour Science* 90:309–323.

Range F., Viranyi Z., Huber L. (2007). "Selective imitation in domestic dogs." *Current Biology* DOI:10.1016.

Range F., Heucke S.L., Gruber C., Konz A., Huber L., Viranyi Z. (2009). "The effect of ostensive cues on dogs' performance in a manipulative social learning task." *Applied Animal Behaviour Science* 120:170–178.

Reid P. (2009). "Adapting to the human world: Dogs' responsiveness to our social cues." *Behavioral Process* 80:325-333.

Slabbert J.M. & Rasa O.A. (1997). "Observational learning of an acquired maternal behaviour pattern by working dog pups: An alternative training method?" *Applied Animal Behavioural Science* 53, 4:309-316.

Smith S.M. & Davis E.S. (2008). "Clicker increases resistance to extinction but does not decrease training time of a simple operant task in domestic dogs (Canis familiaris)." *Applied Animal Behaviour Science* 110:318-329.

Tayler, C. K., and G. S. Saayman (1973) "Imitative Behavior by Indian Ocean Bottlenose Dolphins (Tursiops aduncus) in Captivity." *Behavior* 44:286-98.

Tenaza, R.R.(1976). Songs, choruses and counter singing among Kloss gibbons in Siberutisland, Indonesia. *Zeitschriftfür Tierp* 40:37-52.

Thorpe W.H. (1963). *Learning and Instinct in Animals.* 2nd ed. Cambridge, MA, Harvard University Press.

Topál J., Byrne R.W., Miklósi A., Csanyi V. (2006). "Reproducing human actions and action sequences: "Do As I Do!" in a dog." *Animal Cognition* 9:355–367.

Van de Waal E., Claidière N., Whiten A. (2012). "Social learning and spread of alternatives means of opening an artificial fruit in four groups of vervet monkeys." *Animal Behaviour* 30:1-6 http://dx.doi.org/10.1016/j.anbehav.2012.10.008.

Whiten A. & Custance D. (1996). "Studies in imitation in chimpanzees and children." In Heyes C.M. and Galef B.G. (eds), *Social Learning in Animals: The Roots of Culture.* San Diego: Academic Press 291–318.

Whiten, A., and Ham, R. 1992. "On the nature and evolution of imitation in the animal kingdom: Reappraisal of a century of research." *Adv. Study Behav.* 21: 239 –283

Williams J.L., Friend T.H., Nevill C.H., Archer G. (2004). "The efficacy of a secondary reinforcer (clicker) during acquisition and extinction of an operant task in horses." *Applied Animal Behaviour Science* 88:331–341.

Yoon J.M.D. & Tennie C. (2010). "Contagious yawning: A reflection of empathy, mimicry, or contagion?" *Animal Behaviour* 79, e1e3.

Zentall T.R. (2006). "Imitation: Definition, evidence and mechanisms." *Animal Cognition* 9:335–353.

About the Author

Claudia Fugazza is a Ph.D. candidate in Ethology at Eötvös Lorand University (Budapest). She expects to complete her Ph.D. in the fall of 2014. She is currently conducting research on social learning and imitation in dogs with Dr. Adam Miklósi. She received her B.Sc. in Dog Breeding and Dog Training, a master's in Ethology of Companion Animals and a master's in Dog Training at the University of Pisa (Italy).

Claudia lectures for courses at various universities and master's programs on dog ethology, dog training and social learning in dogs. She also conducts Do As I Do seminars and workshops throughout Europe and the US.

Do As I Do was previously published in Italian, Spanish, German and Russian languages. She has three thesis dissertations: "Social intelligence: a comparison between wolf and dog" (University of Pisa, 2009), "Social learning in dogs as a training technique" (University of Pisa, 2011), and "Ethological analysis of imitation" (University of Pisa, 2011).

Since childhood Claudia Fugazza has been interested in wolf and dog behavior and has grown up with her family's dogs, who taught her to love and respect animals. She lives in Italy, along with her three dogs, Parsifal, Snoopy and Dolly (India has died) with whom she shares much of her free time after all her traveling for research and seminars.

Index

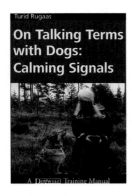

On Talking Terms with Dogs
Calming Signals, 2nd Ed.
Turid Rugaas

Norwegian dog trainer and behaviorist Turid Rugaas is a noted expert on canine body language, notably "calming signals," which are signals dogs use to avoid conflict, invite play, and communicate a wide range of information to other dogs and people. These are the dogs' attempt to defuse situations that otherwise might result in fights or aggression.

Companion DVD, *Calming Signals: What Your Dog Tells You,* is also available. The DVD shows footage of many calming signals, how dogs use them, and how you can use them to calm your dog.

Play Together, Stay Together
Happy and Healthy Play Between People and Dogs
Patricia McConnell and Karen London

Play is powerful stuff, and it has a profound influence on your relationship with your dog. Learn how to read your dog's play-cues and how to teach him some charming tricks to wow your friends. Play gives your dog mental and physical exercise and builds the bond between the two of you. If you'd like a happier, more responsive dog and a closer relationship with each other, then this booklet is for you.

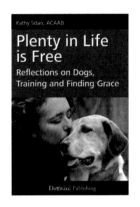

Plenty in Life is Free
Reflections on Dogs, Training and Finding Grace
Kathy Sdao

In *Plenty in Life is Free,* renowned dog trainer Kathy Sdao reveals how her journey through life and her decades of experience training marine mammals and dogs led her to reject a number of sacred cows including the leadership model of dog training. She describes in narrative fashion how she has come to focus her own training philosophy which emphasizes developing partnerships in which humans and dogs exchange reinforcements and continually cede the upper hand to one another.

Positive Perspectives
Love Your Dog, Train Your Dog
Pat Miller

A complete dog training, puppy raising, problem solving, and basic health guide. Written as a series of columns in "Whole Dog Journal", *Positive Perspectives* gives you information on day-to-day living with dogs in small easily understood "bites". Find out how to prevent problems before they occur, train without force with fun and treats, learn about the newest vaccination schedules and much more to live happily with your dog. For puppy as well as adult dog owners.

Dogwise.com is your source for quality books, ebooks, DVDs, training tools and treats.

We've been selling to the dog fancier for more than 25 years and we carefully screen our products for quality information, safety, durability and FUN! You'll find something for every level of dog enthusiast on our website, www.dogwise.com, or drop by our store in Wenatchee, Washington.

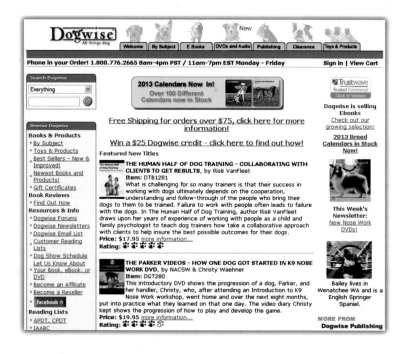